This is the second book in a series designed to aid in the fostering of acceptance and understanding of transgender individuals, more specifically in children who may or do have a trans* person in their life. The first book, My New Mommy, published in August 2012, dealt with male to female transition. This book explains, in simple terms, female to male transition. Though the re-titling of a parent is something that is as private a decision as transition itself, the use of "Daddy" and "Mommy" here are more strictly to explain the mental acceptance of Charles, our little narrator, then to indicate the need for such a title change.

ACKNOWLEDGMENTS

To list all the names of those that have assisted with the making of this book, from conception on would create a whole new book. So for those who are not mentioned, you have not been forgotten. Your support has been tremendous.

In particularly....

Sage Mossiano: without my illustrator and partner, I would be lost.

Mom and Dad: without the both of you supporting me and being there for me through this process, I would not have made it this far.

Adrian Michael: without your assistance, I never would have made it this far.

Philip Tolliver: without your assistance, and your expertise, I never would have made my deadlines.

My New Daddy

Written by Lilly Mossiano

Illustrated by Sage Mossiano

Published by Spun Silver Productions
spunsilverproductions.com

ISBN: 1484817222
ISBN-13: 978-1484817223

Foreword

It is my great pleasure to write the foreword to this short, but fantastic book. When I first signed on to help Ms. Mossiano with My New Mommy in 2012, I had no idea this book was in the works. She let me read the manuscript, and I was stunned by the simplicity and the emotions it raised in me. You see, I was in the closet. A man, trapped in a woman's body, trapped in a deep and dark closet. This book gave me the strength to step out as myself, and work towards being an advocate for FtM parents everywhere. I know that this book will aid my son in understanding why he has two male parents, and I know it will help FtM people everywhere.

This short illustrated work is designed to explain FtM transition to children between 4 and 8 years of age, but can be used in any teaching capacity to foster understand and acceptance in society. The time has come to make the change so desperately needed. This book is the first of its kind, and a great tool to be used to achieve that goal.

Enjoy and spread the word!

Best Regards,

Adrian Michael Van Slaars

For my nephew, Nolan, may this aid you in answering all your questions.

Hi, my name is Charles, and this is what my mommy used to look like.

She use to have long hair, then one day we went to the barber, and she got it cut short.

Then one day, my mommy took me to get a new bike. She also bought one, so she could go riding with me.

It looked a lot like mine. It was even the same color.

My mommy sat down with me and explained to me that nature made a mistake and she should have been born a boy like me.

After our talk, my mommy started buying men's clothes, and dressing like a daddy. She also started going by a new name, and I started calling her daddy.

My daddy went to go see Doctor Voltaire, so that he could start looking more and more like a daddy and less like a mommy.

After some time, my new daddy went to the see Doctor Voltaire again. He needed to have an operation to make him become a boy like me.

Now I am a lucky little boy because my mommy is my new daddy. He will always love me and I will always love him.

Being transgender in today's society can be challenging. Without a lot of education or tolerance being taught, gender nonconforming individuals often find themselves in uncomfortable and often dangerous situations.

Below are resources to aid transgender and other gender nonconforming individuals in their journey. Some are support groups, others are law groups and advocacy centers that can help with discrimination cases and hate crimes.

You are **not** alone.

Transgender Resources:

Susan's Place: http://www.susans.org

GLAAD: http://www.glaad.org/transgender

PFLAG: http:// www. pflag .org

Human Rights Campaign: http://www.hrc.org/issues/transgender

The Transgender Law Center: http://transgenderlawcenter.org/

Wipe Out Transphobia: http://wipeouttransphobia.com

Lilly Mossiano is the author of My New Mommy and My New Daddy. She is an LGBT advocate, and a geek at heart. She is a fan of horror and sci-fi genres. She is currently working on several young adult and older children's books in those categories, as well as expanding the "My New" Series to include siblings and other family members, as well as address the other parents in My New Mommy and My New Daddy.

She lives in North Carolina with her wife and partner, Sage Mossiano.
You can find her on the following sites:

Facebook: http://www.facebook.com/LillyMossiano
Website: http://lillymossiano.wordpress.com